God bl... ...e +

Tom + Jill Bomberger

One-Minute Prayers™

FOR MY
Son

HARVEST HOUSE PUBLISHERS

EUGENE, OREGON

Cover by Garborg Design Works, Minneapolis, Minnesota

Cover photo © Angus Plummer / iStockphoto.com

ONE-MINUTE PRAYERS™ FOR MY SON
Copyright © 2006 by Harvest House Publishers
Published by Harvest House Publishers
Eugene, Oregon 97402
www.harvesthousepublishers.com

ONE-MINUTE PRAYERS is a series trademark of The Hawkins Children's LLC. Harvest House Publishers, Inc., is the exclusive licensee of the trademark ONE-MINUTE PRAYERS.

ISBN-13: 978-0-7369-1616-5
ISBN-10: 0-7369-1616-4

Printed in the United States of America

06 07 08 09 10 11 12 13 14 / BP-MS / 10 9 8 7 6 5 4 3 2 1

Contents

Listen, my son, to your father's instruction and do not forsake your mother's teaching. They will be a garland to grace your head and a chain to adorn your neck.

PROVERBS 1:8-9

Birth

Known

The word of the LORD came to me, saying,
"Before I formed you in the womb I knew you,
before you were born I set you apart; I appointed
you as a prophet to the nations."

JEREMIAH 1:4-5

Before I memorized the profile of his face captured in a sonogram, before I understood the joy he would bring to the family, before I held him in my arms, You knew my son. You knew of his strengths and weaknesses. You knew my son would bite his lip when tired and hug me with the fierceness of pure love.

Lord, You formed my son's beautiful face and soul before I met him face-to-face. Teach me all about my son and the path You have for him. His birth has delivered him into my care—may I help lead him into Your presence for eternity.

Family

Speaking of the Future

Who am I, O LORD God, and what is my family, that
you have brought me this far? And as if this were not
enough in your sight, O God, you have spoken about
the future of the house of your servant.

1 CHRONICLES 17:16-17

Lord, not only have You provided me with love and
a family, You also speak about a future hope. I see it in
my son's life and am grateful every day. Truly, You do
not limit Your goodness and grace to one generation,
but create a legacy of faith in every family willing to
embrace it.

Hear my prayers for my child's life and future. I
know he is in Your care. You have brought him this far,
and I have peace that You will speak words of future and
promise into his life just as You have done in mine.

The Long View

The plans of the LORD stand firm forever,
the purposes of his heart through all generations.

PSALM 33:11

How reassuring, Lord, to know Your plans stand firm! No parent–son battle of wills, no failing of understanding, no "wrong side of the bed" day can thwart Your purpose for my son and our family and Your larger vision for this struggling world.

What an amazing gift to be able to lean into Your grace and Your faithfulness, knowing You will use this very raw material—one parent and one son—to make Your ways known to all generations.

For the Lonely

God sets the lonely in families,
he leads forth the prisoners with singing;
but the rebellious live in a sun-scorched land.

PSALM 68:6

Grown-ups don't have the corner on loneliness. I've seen that already with my son. A child easily feels left out of things. Adult conversations. Playground groups. A difficult lesson in class. When my son feels lonely, remind him of Your promises, God. Free him from the unfruitful thoughts that can trap him in despair or make him doubt his purpose.

Thank You for the hubbub of families, Lord. With family, we always know we're part of something, even when we are feeling distant and out of sorts. I pray my son does not experience the long, dry times of the truly rebellious. Remind him he is never, ever alone if he looks to You, Lord. He will always find family in his Father's house.

A Personal Prayer for My Son

Love

He Will Know

A new command I give you: Love one another.
As I have loved you, so you must love one another.
By this all men will know that you are my disciples,
if you love one another.

JOHN 13:34-35

I know Your love deeply and personally. Lord, does my son see and feel love's example in our home? I pray I would model Your heart as much as possible. I pray I would love my child unconditionally and with depth and strength so he will know You.

When I am not the encourager my son needs, please guide me toward better ways. And when we both need to draw from You, the source of love, to refresh our spirits and live strong, may we never hesitate to call on Your name.

Impossible Love

*Love is patient, love is kind. It does not envy, it does
not boast, it is not proud. It is not rude, it is not self-
seeking, it is not easily angered, it keeps no record
of wrongs.*

1 CORINTHIANS 13:4-5

What do you mean, God, when You give us this
impossible list? My son is sometimes willful and impatient. He has a long memory for perceived injustices.
He wants everything now and at no personal cost…he
is just like me.

No stubborn march toward good behavior will get
my son, myself, to this Love. We will have to take the
bridge—Your Son, standing in the gap for us. Help my
son have the eyes to see what You have given me to
see—glimmerings of impossible love in the day-to-day
workings of this imperfect but perfected family.

How Do We Know?

If anyone obeys his word, God's love is truly made
complete in him. This is how we know we are in
him: Whoever claims to live in him must walk as
Jesus did.

1 JOHN 2:5-6

"How do you know?" my son asks of matters large
and small. The simplest of evidence reassures him.
Help me, Lord, make use of this precious time. A time
when my son truly possesses what Christ held most
dear—the heart of a child.

Confirm in my son's heart Your love in him and
for him. Help me demonstrate a life of obedience and
compassion—the kind of walk that cannot be born of
will, only of Your presence. Thank You, Lord, for the
power in a child's conviction and for Your promise of
completion.

A Personal Prayer
for My Son

Health

Home Remedy

Do not be wise in your own eyes;
fear the LORD and shun evil.
This will bring health to your body
and nourishment to your bones.

PROVERBS 3:7-8

So many dangers exist in the world. I need only watch the news one night to be overcome with fear about my child's welfare. I realize how much I depend on You to protect my son. Direct the path of my child so he would stay clear of danger and evil purposes. Fill him with the nourishment and wisdom of the Spirit so he can stand firm in his faith.

Lord, I know I cannot always be the one to watch over my son. Give me the strength I need now to begin entrusting You with his safety and care. Your eyes never leave him—and I pray his eyes will never wander from Your loving face.

Order Up

*Restore to me the joy of your salvation
and grant me a willing spirit, to sustain me.*

PSALM 51:12

My son's idea of sustenance is a meal in a colorful box delivered through the car window.

As he needs my help to eat properly, he needs You, Lord, to sustain him with spiritual food.

I pray as my son moves through his life, You will quicken his spirit to remember the "good stuff." Give him a hunger for the joy and wholeness that comes from a willing spirit attuned to You.

Who Was That Masked Man?

The man who was healed had no idea who it was, for Jesus had slipped away into the crowd that was there.

JOHN 5:13

You heal us in so many ways, Lord. Spiritually, physically, emotionally. Throughout his life, I pray my son will remember to attribute every good thing to You. Unlike the man who didn't know who healed him, let my son's first thought go to You when he is restored in some way. Likewise, let him seek You when he needs healing.

But there is yet another lesson here, Lord. Write it on my son's heart: Acts of kindness and grace don't have to be showy and be applauded to be miracles.

A Personal Prayer for My Son

Friends

A Heart for Others

*My intercessor is my friend
as my eyes pour out tears to God;
on behalf of a man he pleads with God
as a man pleads for his friend.*

JOB 16:20-21

The precious prayers from a child's lips bring me back to the basics of faith, Lord. We are supposed to love and care for others. We have hearts made for compassion. Give my child a prayerful spirit so that he would turn his concerns and those of his friends over to You daily. I long to hear him speak of the wonders You have done in his life.

You, Lord, can turn a little boy into a prayer warrior. Lead us as a family to our knees so that we might raise up a mighty man of God who prays on behalf of those in need and those he calls friends.

Forever Friends

I am a friend to all who fear you,
to all who follow your precepts.
The earth is filled with your love, O LORD;
teach me your decrees.

PSALM 119:63-64

A godly friend is a priceless gift, but sometimes this realization is hard-won. As my son goes out into the world—away from me for hours at first, then days, then years—help him seek out those who know You and respect Your ways. Encourage him to uphold Your precepts and count among his friends those who honor You.

The earth is filled with evidence of You. Let my son be a seeker—one who looks for You in everyone he meets and who exhibits You in all his actions. A good friend. A godly man.

After You

*Be devoted to one another in brotherly love. Honor
one another above yourselves.*

ROMANS 12:10

Lord, help my son look beyond himself to care for
and honor others first. Selflessness cannot be taught. It
needs to be experienced. I pray my son would know,
at a young age, the quiet joy that comes from showing
others the love and kindness Your Son shows us.

Guide my young man to exhibit Your kind of love
to his family and friends. Keep him from being deterred
when the world does not answer in kind. May Your
Holy Spirit, not the spirit of this age, be his guide.

A Personal Prayer
for My Son

Future

The Beginning of Forever

In the beginning you laid the foundations of the
earth, and the heavens are the work of your hands...
Like clothing you will change them and they will
be discarded. But you remain the same, and your
years will never end. The children of your servants
will live in your presence; their descendants will be
established before you.

PSALM 102:25-28

The hands that formed the foundations of the earth
and the universe formed the body and mind and spirit
of my child. I do not forget this. How can I? Every day
I see glimpses of who he is deep inside. When I try
to recognize which parent he reminds me of most, I
realize he is unique and wonderfully made to resemble
his heavenly Father.

Father, You remain the same. I take great delight
in this knowledge, because my child will always have
his Creator, his Maker to call upon. Bring my son—the
child You knew from the very beginning—into Your
presence for eternity.

The Big Picture

*There is surely a future hope for you,
and your hope will not be cut off.*

PROVERBS 23:18

My son has already experienced dashed hopes. It rains on game day. A much-desired toy falls short of its advertised glory. A friend does not keep a promise. In a world that values the short-term and disposable, I pray You give my son a vision for the long view.

May he know all his days are secure in You. May his hopes and actions be in accord with Your plans for him. May he live his days comforted by Your presence and Your unfailing, eternal promises.

Doing Away with Worry

Do not worry about tomorrow, for tomorrow will worry about itself. Each day has enough trouble of its own.

MATTHEW 6:34

❧

Nothing disturbs a parent's heart like the worries of a child. My son's troubles and concerns become my own as I strive to offer him perspective and comfort. How often I fail!

Lord, when my son's busy mind clutches at and feeds his worries, please send him Your embracing peace. Let him experience the present with a clear mind and with Your promises in mind. Take away his thoughts of tomorrow's troubles and replace them with Your assurances for today.

A Personal Prayer for My Son

Wisdom

Wanting the Right Thing

Flee the evil desires of youth, and pursue righteous-ness, faith, love and peace, along with those who call on the Lord out of a pure heart.

2 TIMOTHY 2:22

Lord, thank You for Your complete knowledge of my son. In Your Word You acknowledge the desires of youth. Nothing is lost on You. This is a lesson it is never too early to learn.

In a world that makes evil look so good, give my son the desire for a pure heart. Give him a heart that runs toward righteousness and calls out for Your guidance. Equip him with the courage to walk away from the inevitable temptations of youth—to not take his cues from the crowd but from You, the One who made him, knows him, and loves him completely.

Known Quantity

*Walk in all the way that the L*ORD *your God has com-*
manded you, so that you may live and prosper and
prolong your days in the land that you will possess.

DEUTERONOMY 5:33

Lord, I pray my son would walk with You all his
days. May he follow Your commands and enjoy a long
life, prosperous in the important things—rich friend-
ships, a loving family life, fulfilling work, and the contentment that comes from knowing You deeply.

Quicken my son's spirit to recognize the wisdom
of Your commands and to appreciate the untarnished
spiritual wealth of a life lived obedient to Your Word.

Teachable Moments

Teach me your way, O LORD,
and I will walk in your truth;
give me an undivided heart,
that I may fear your name.

PSALM 86:11

Sometimes, Lord, I wish I could download the life lessons I've learned and give my son instant access to them. But his walk with You will be a journey, as mine has been. There will be teachable moments and regrettable stumbles.

Give my son an undivided heart. When he comes to a crossroads, make Your way clear to him. Teach him to respect Your truth and call upon Your fearsome name in all things, confident You will draw alongside him all his days.

A Personal Prayer for My Son

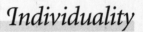

Individuality

Count Him Blessed

*The very hairs of your head are all numbered.
Don't be afraid; you are worth more than many
sparrows.*

LUKE 12:7

How good to know there is another who feels as I
do—that the very hairs of my son's head are precious
and unique in all the world. I pray my son would grow
to see his worth centered in You, so that no man can
rob him of the compassionate confidence Your love
inspires.

The smallest sparrow does not escape Your notice.
Thank You, Creator God, for the unmerited love You
show us as individuals. Thank You for counting my
son's every hair, every breath. Thank You for counting
him as Your own.

Mindful of the Maker

*I praise you because I am fearfully
and wonderfully made;
your works are wonderful,
I know that full well.*

PSALM 139:14

What an amazing thing is this body, this person, my son! May he never take for granted Your wonderful workmanship, Lord. Let him grow up strong and secure and offer praise to You for the unshakable evidence of Your care. Allow him to recognize and know full well the works of You, the Master Designer.

May I also fully understand that my life is a miracle shaped by Your hands. I know You love me. On days when I feel like an unfit parent or a misguided adult, keep me in the knowledge of Your grace and care.

God's Talented and Gifted Program

Each man has his own gift from God; one has this gift, another has that.

1 CORINTHIANS 7:7

The comparisons start so early. When I see my son taking note of others' talents and strengths and measuring them against his own, I am so grateful for Your words, Lord: "One has this gift, another has that."

Help my son recognize and honor You as the source of all gifts. I pray he wouldn't engage in hurtful bragging or, conversely, value himself less because he lacks another's gift. Let him always be quick to see the God-given qualities in everyone he meets.

A Personal Prayer
for My Son

Strength

When It Hurts

*Consider it pure joy, my brothers, whenever you face
trials of many kinds, because you know that the
testing of your faith develops perseverance.*

JAMES 1:2-4

It's so difficult to see my son endure trials. The
smallest slight is wounding and, for him, sometimes
bewildering. Lord, when my son faces troubles large
and small, teach him to persevere, secure in the knowledge he is never alone. Comfort his spirit with Your
Holy Spirit. Without Your grace, joy and pain are irra-
tional companions—only You can bring the former
from the latter. When he is tested, I pray my son would
see past the obstacle to the opportunity—the chance
to grow in faith and his knowledge of You.

Standing Strong

Be strong and courageous. Do not be afraid or ter-
rified because of them, for the LORD your God goes
with you; he will never leave you nor forsake you.

DEUTERONOMY 31:6

Strength and courage are familiar traits to my son, a fan of comic superheroes and a victor over imaginary villains. But when he meets up with real foes—physical or spiritual ones—I pray he would look to You, Lord. And not just for backup.

May You be my son's first source for guidance in difficult situations. May he stand firm in his convictions and not fear those who want him to fail. Fortify his walk with You, so he may have unshakable confidence in Your promise: You will never leave him.

Youth Matters

*Don't let anyone look down on you because you
are young, but set an example for the believers in
speech, in life, in love, in faith and in purity.*

1 TIMOTHY 4:12

When my son says his nightly prayer, it has tan-
gents and postscripts. He thanks You for ants, asks
for math help, and expresses concern for thin, hungry
children he sees on TV. He has supreme confidence
You are hanging on every word.

And You are. Maintain in him this simple, powerful
faith—pure, cleanly spoken, and childlike in its trust.
Let him be a blessing to other believers and an example
for those who do not yet know You.

A Personal Prayer
for My Son

Happiness

Psst...Have You Heard?

*I have learned the secret of being content in any
and every situation, whether well fed or hungry,
whether living in plenty or in want. I can do everything through him who gives me strength.*

PHILIPPIANS 4:12-13

Young boys love a good secret. The secret to contentment is one I pray my son would hear and take
to heart. Reveal to him in youth that, regardless of
circumstances, he will find steady joy in You, the One
who gives him strength.

And Lord, let my son be a poor secret-keeper!
Whether poor or rich, make him bold in stating the
source of his contentment. Let his actions and his attitude be a constant witness for You.

I Love You—Pass It On

If you obey my commands, you will remain in my love, just as I have obeyed my Father's commands and remain in his love. I have told you this so that my joy may be in you and that your joy may be complete. My command is this: Love each other as I have loved you.

JOHN 15:10-12

When my son obeys and respects me I'm on cloud nine. When he is rebellious I grieve. When he says, "I don't like you anymore," I say, "I love you." It's a hard thing to argue with.

But You know that, Lord. Your supreme command is also Your supreme gift. You offer Your incalculable love and then remain with us as we sputter and mutter and finally admit there's nothing left to say except, "I love You, too." Thank You, Lord, for commanding us to do the one thing that makes and keeps us whole.

Appreciating Assets

When God gives any man wealth and possessions, and enables him to enjoy them, to accept his lot and be happy in his work—this is a gift of God. He seldom reflects on the days of his life, because God keeps him occupied with gladness of heart.

ECCLESIASTES 5:19-20

My son enjoys the present. He doesn't have much use for the past. The future is a vague place where birthdays and Christmases hang out. Give him a couple of buddies and some "now" to work with, and he is one happy camper.

Lord, seal this quality in his character. Don't let him outgrow it, as so many of us do. Contentment with current riches is such a very holy gift. Help me, as a parent, point to You in gratitude for all that we have as a family this very day.

A Personal Prayer
for My Son

Respect

Respect for the Right Reasons

Children, obey your parents in the Lord, for this is right. "Honor your father and mother"—which is the first commandment with a promise—"that it may go well with you and that you may enjoy long life on the earth."

EPHESIANS 6:1-3

Father God, help my son respect me for the right reasons. Not just "because I and God say so," but because he recognizes the good things that come of it—peace in the household, an environment of security, and a genuine willingness to help one another.

I pray these early lessons in respect would yield results all my son's life. Let his friends, his employers, and his future wife see You in the honorable way he treats them.

Thank You, Lord, for setting the ultimate example for parents. Thank You for showing us we must temper commands with compassion and love.

Wise Guy

He who listens to a life-giving rebuke
will be at home among the wise.

PROVERBS 15:31

Sometimes I correct my son out of anger and impatience. Sometime my rebukes are thoughtful and necessary. How is he to know which reproofs are life-giving?

Lord, make us both sensitive to Your spirit. Quicken my son's conscience when a rebuke requires a change of behavior. When my correction stems from something other than a desire for my son's well-being, silence me. Then we can both be at home among the wise.

Falling Up

The Lord upholds all those who fall
and lifts up all who are bowed down.

PSALM 145:14

Lord, watching my son, I realize how humbling childhood is. It's the chapter full of scraped knees, runny noses, and hurt feelings. It's the time when a boy is expected to pick himself up and try again.

Thank You for upholding my son when he falls, Father God. Thank You for respecting the small pains of youth and for helping with the larger ones of adulthood. When my son is bowed with troubles, lift his head so he can praise the One who sees, understands, and heals.

A Personal Prayer
for My Son

Safety

Rock of Ages

*Your faithfulness continues through all generations;
you established the earth, and it endures.*

PSALM 119:90

Lord, the Earth gets a lot of attention around our house. Rocks collect on shelves. Dirt comes in as mud pies or on sneakers. Spiders receive daring rescues. My son loves the physical world You created. He turns to it like a reliable companion. It's the bedrock of his days.

Stir in my son the same delight for the things of Your Spirit, Creator God. Enfold him in Your quiet presence so he would feel protected and comforted. Show him that the One who made stones, oceans, and trees abides with *him* as well, as constant as the flow of generations, as constant as the Earth.

Delighting in the Light

Love does not delight in evil but rejoices with the truth. It always protects, always trusts, always hopes, always perseveres.

1 CORINTHIANS 13:6-7

I wish I could say my son never delights in evil, but that's not the case. It's our human nature, at times, to take pleasure in seeing someone we don't like get their due. Or to deliver a comment that leaves its mark on another.

Lord, help me teach my son to love as You love. Turn his thoughts to kindness so that he would never choose to be cruel. Protect him from being a victim of cruelty. Give him a nature of trust and hope so his compassion for others wouldn't waver or depend on consequences. Fill my son with Your light, so he would shine as an example of one who loves You.

Benediction for My Boy

*The LORD will keep you from all harm—he will
watch over your life; the LORD will watch over your
coming and going both now and forevermore.*

PSALM 121:7-8

The words of this psalm are a parent's prayer, Lord.
What a comfort they are! Protect my son from harm.
Watch over him when I cannot. Guide his steps as he
tries new things. Temper his pride and bravado when
he thinks he's got life all figured out. Teach him to
recognize that evil finds a home in attitudes as well
as deeds.

Right now, my son is in my home and I can watch
over, instruct, and admonish him. But when I'm honest
with myself, I know my love is not enough. How we
need You, my son and I. Thank You for Your protection, promised now and forevermore.

A Personal Prayer
for My Son

Play

Hearing Your Song

Let them praise his name with dancing and make music to him with tambourine and harp.

PSALM 149:3

I love to watch my son dance. Even as a toddler, he would hear a drumbeat and work up a wobbly groove. It wasn't something he'd learned, it was just part of him—an expression of pure joy.

I pray my son would show You the same unguarded response when he feels Your presence or recognizes Your handiwork. All his life, let him praise You with his words, songs, and deeds.

Seek, Find, Rejoice

Glory in his holy name;
let the hearts of those who seek the LORD rejoice.

1 CHRONICLES 16:10

Half the fun of hide-and-seek is in the seeking—counting slowly, listening for clues, thinking of new hiding spots. Then the reward—that *aha* moment of surprise, that thrill when the seeker and the sought connect.

Make my son a lifetime seeker of You, Lord. Not in the sense of always looking for You, but in wanting to discover new things about You and deepening his walk with You. May he seek out Your full nature, the meaning of all Your names. I pray my son would rejoice in those precious moments of connection that refresh our faith and make our relationship with You ever new.

Exclamation Points!

Our mouths were filled with laughter,
our tongues with songs of joy.
Then it was said among the nations,
"The LORD has done great things for them."
The LORD has done great things for us,
and we are filled with joy.

PSALM 126:2-3

I love this psalm. It makes me smile to read it. It reminds me of a child, Lord. When my son is excited about something, he bounces, shouts, points. He's not stingy with his experience. He wants everyone around him to not just *know* what he's talking about, but to *feel* it. Look! Can you believe that? This is *so* cool!

Lord, I pray my son would have moments like these in his spiritual life. Fill him with joy and praise and let him be eager to tell everyone its source. Thank You for Your Word, showing us this side of worship—the playful, exclamation-filled side of being Yours.

A Personal Prayer
for My Son

Education

The Real Education

God is exalted in his power.
Who is a teacher like him?

JOB 36:22

When my son said his first word, I was so proud.
There was a part of me that delighted in his genius. I
couldn't wait to tell others. Of course, I cannot really
take credit, but it is fun to revel in each achievement.
I consider how You will teach my son the most important life lessons of all. And when he discovers what it
means to serve, to pray, to follow Your will, You will
be glorified.

His life is in Your hands. His spiritual education
began the day he was born. There is no greater teacher
than his Creator, and I am grateful.

A Ready Pupil

Good and upright is the LORD;
therefore he instructs sinners in his ways.
He guides the humble in what is right
and teaches them his way.

PSALM 25:8-9

Lord, give my son a willing and humble spirit. May he always be open to Your teachings and wisdom. I pray that nothing he is taught by me and others would interfere with all the knowledge You want to bestow upon him.

My hope is that his teachers and those who are leaders in his life will always teach him what is right and good. Guard his heart from false teachings, and renew his mind and spirit so he always would be eager to learn from You.

Turning

Train a child in the way he should go,
and when he is old he will not turn from it.

PROVERBS 22:6

My son always squirms when he gets impatient. I reach for his arm in a supermarket, and he turns nearly inside out to get away from my grasp. When I am instructing him, he likes to turn and focus on something else. Help me raise him so he would not turn from You and Your wisdom.

Lord, I will teach my son Your way. And for now, I can only pray that when You reach for him in later years, he and his heart would not turn away from truth.

A Personal Prayer
for My Son

Prayer

Real Prayers

When you pray, do not be like the hypocrites, for they love to pray standing in the synagogues and on the street corners to be seen by men. I tell you the truth, they have received their reward in full. But when you pray, go into your room, close the door and pray to your Father, who is unseen. Then your Father, who sees what is done in secret, will reward you.

MATTHEW 6:5-7

Somewhere along the way, my son learned how to tell me what I wanted to hear. It works for a while to keep everyone happy, but eventually he loses sight of the truth. I'm sure I learned the same habit at a very young age. Amazingly, this can become so true for our prayer lives. We offer up lofty words or perfectly phrased requests and praises—and lose the heart of the truth. We lose the intimate relationship You offer us.

Give my son a heart that speaks truthfully when in Your presence. May he not try to use the right words, but the right spirit. And grant him a humble attitude, so he would never be walking a false faith for the sake of appearances, but always be striving for authentic dialogue with his Creator.

Opinionated

God exalted him to the highest place
and gave him the name that is above every name,
that at the name of Jesus every knee should bow,
in heaven and on earth and under the earth,
and every tongue confess that Jesus Christ is Lord,
to the glory of God the Father.

PHILIPPIANS 2:9-11

Getting a confession out of a young boy often involves promises of treats. But to get a young boy to profess something, is not so hard. Amazingly, he has formed opinions about many things, including what is on television, what is served at dinner, and how You created the universe. I pray there would always be room in my son's very strong mind and spirit to be tender toward his confession of faith and submissive when he stands before You each day.

May his prayers always lead him to his knees so that You might raise him up with the confidence of faith in who You are—Lord of all.

Love's Return

I will give them a heart to know me, that I am the LORD. *They will be my people, and I will be their God, for they will return to me with all their heart.*

JEREMIAH 24:7

The world preaches that we should always get something for our efforts, for our attempts at kindness and goodness, for our labor. Our return for leading a life of faith is that we can always return to Your embrace. We know our way home because You have shown us the path. We might not always be great at the Christian walk, but we can always strive to know You better.

I pray that my son would always be prayerful, even during times of doubt or trouble, so that he might understand fully the reward of faith—to be loved as Your child.

A Personal Prayer
for My Son

Purpose

Your Blessing

He will bless the fruit of your womb, the crops of your land—your grain, new wine and oil—the calves of your herds and the lambs of your flocks in the land that he swore to your forefathers to give you.

DEUTERONOMY 7:13

As much as I worry about my son—as much as I try to make his life better—I know it is Your blessing upon his life that will bring him purpose and fulfillment. I need not worry about every detail of his existence, his day, his future, because they are all in Your hands.

Lord, may You hold and bless my son in the years to come. May his life be good and holy and pleasing in Your sight. Give him a purpose, a calling. And may all that he is and has be under Your covering.

In All Things

We know that in all things God works for the good of those who love him, who have been called according to his purpose.

ROMANS 8:28

It is difficult to explain life, faith, and purpose to a child. I have tried on several occasions to convey a sense of You to my son. I realize much of his faith education will need to come from living and experiencing You on a daily basis. There will be times when he fails or stumbles and cannot find his way. There will be other times when he clearly sees the way to go and his actions are sure and good.

I pray my son would learn to give all things over to Your care so that the trials and the victories and the times of doubt would all be used for Your purpose.

You Are There

My dear friends, as you have always obeyed—not only in my presence, but now much more in my absence—continue to work out your salvation with fear and trembling, for it is God who works in you to will and to act according to his good purpose.

PHILIPPIANS 2:12-14

Kids grow up. As much as I don't want this to happen—on some level—I am excited to see my child become a man. There will likely be times when we are miles and miles apart either emotionally or geographically. It is then I will need to radically exercise my faith in Your constant presence.

Even when I am not there to offer encouragement or guidance, You are. When I realize I am meddling or being overbearing and need to step back, You will be working in my son's heart and life to shape his days to Your good purpose. May I always know when to let go of my son, and may my son always know when to hold tightly to You.

A Personal Prayer
for My Son

Trust

It's a Matter of Trust

Trust in the LORD and do good;
dwell in the land and enjoy safe pasture.
Delight yourself in the LORD
and he will give you the desires of your heart.

PSALM 37:3-4

I pray my child would always take delight in loving
You. His laughter nearly brings me to tears—tears of
joy and gratefulness. I know his trusting faith must
give You the same pleasure.

I want the best for my child. May he receive the
desires of his heart...and may his heart always desire
to know Yours better.

Living

When I am afraid,
I will trust in you.
In God, whose word I praise,
in God I trust; I will not be afraid.
What can mortal man do to me?

PSALM 56:3-4

Lord, am I showing my son how to trust in You? Sometimes my fretting gets in the way of the message I want him to hear—that You are in charge and we are able to trust You completely. When my fear overrides Your mercy, give my son the heart to see beyond my humanness. Let the trust of a child never be broken or belittled.

Give me confidence and courage to live a life of trust. I want to model the ways of faith for my son. I want him to never choose fear over living.

A Confident Faith

Trust in the LORD with all your heart
and lean not on your own understanding;
in all your ways acknowledge him,
and he will make your paths straight.

PROVERBS 3:5-6

I can see it in his eyes—his deep need to do things on his own, without my help. To go from holding a totally dependent child to facing off with a defiant son is so frustrating. How does someone adjust to this change? Lord, at times like this I must turn to prayer. I ask You to protect him from his own will.

God, govern the heart and mind of my son. May he seek and trust Your understanding and knowledge in all situations. Take hold of his wandering path and make it straight so that it would not present him with detours but a clear way toward Your truth.

A Personal Prayer
for My Son

Diligence

Goal

*One thing I do: Forgetting what is behind and
straining toward what is ahead, I press on toward
the goal to win the prize for which God has called
me heavenward in Christ Jesus.*

PHILIPPIANS 3:13-14

Kids can be so focused on sports and sporting
events. At a young age they taste the sweetness of victory and the bitterness of defeat. What will my son do
when the stakes are higher and the potential loss so
much greater in real life?

I pray for him to have a disciplined heart that
knows the value of pressing on even when there is
not an immediate goal in sight. When he experiences
defeat, carry him, Lord. When he savors triumph, may
he glorify You.

Because I Said So

Discipline your son, and he will give you peace;
he will bring delight to your soul.

PROVERBS 29:17

This parenting thing is not easy. I always thought I would be comfortable with the disciplining of my son. But I am finding it more and more difficult to be strong in my stance. I look to Your role in my life. I have always felt the comfort of Your unwavering strength. I have rested in knowing You do not change Your mind with the shift of mood or circumstance.

Lord, help me be that source of comfort and strength to my son. Help my son learn the security of abiding by the rules when they are created to protect him. May his life give You delight and honor as he discovers the goodness in doing right…not because I said so, but because You call us to goodness.

What's for Sale?

Buy the truth and do not sell it;
get wisdom, discipline and understanding.

PROVERBS 23:23

Everybody has something to sell these days. Some things look so shiny and wonderful that passing them by seems impossible, crazy, a missed opportunity. God, I want my son to have a discerning heart. I pray he would quicken his steps when he approaches those selling lies or misfortune. And may he stop and pay attention when truth is presented to him.

What he discards and what he keeps will be up to him. But, Lord…I pray You would guide him in these choices. My hope is for him to hold tightly to wisdom, discipline, and understanding—for these lead to true wealth.

A Personal Prayer
for My Son

Character

The Path to Character

We...rejoice in our sufferings, because we know
that suffering produces perseverance; perseverance,
character; and character, hope.

ROMANS 5:3-4

There is a whole lot of whining going on in our
home these days. Sometimes I worry about the work
ethic of today's child. How all of us want the road
paved smooth and safe and guaranteed to reach the
destination we want. But the speed bumps, potholes,
and detours are sometimes exactly what we need in
order to grow in godly character.

Remind me, Father, to be an example of perseverance the next time we sit for endless minutes in the
middle of a traffic jam. If we fall into financial trouble,
encourage me to turn it into a lesson of trusting Your
provision. Direct us all to the hope of living the Christian life.

In Good Company

Do not be misled: "Bad company corrupts good character."

1 CORINTHIANS 15:33

Lead my son to the company of those who love You, Lord. Wrap the arms of Christian community around my child as he becomes a man. Deter him from seeking companionship and friendship among those who do not follow Your way.

Give me insight as I teach my son right from wrong. Grant us both a sense of understanding as we relate to other people. Allow us grace to forgive and also wisdom to set boundaries. Protect the character of my child so that his life is a blessing to You.

Batteries Not Required

Whoever lives by the truth comes into the light, so that it may be seen plainly that what he has done has been done through God.

JOHN 3:21

A life driven by the light of the Lord does not need any other source of energy or passion to forge ahead. I pray that my son's character would be firmly planted in the identity of Christ so that the light of righteousness would shine from his heart and onto the path before him.

May his feet be firmly grounded in Your Word so that each decision he makes would align with Your will for him. My son's success in life, his happiness, and his maturing in character will be made possible when he steps into the warmth of Your love and the matchless truth of Your light.

A Personal Prayer
for My Son

Attitude

Change in Attitude

*You were taught, with regard to your former way
of life, to put off your old self, which is being cor-
rupted by its deceitful desires; to be made new in
the attitude of your minds; and to put on the new
self, created to be like God in true righteousness
and holiness.*

EPHESIANS 4:22-24

∽

There are days when I worry about my son's attitude. Where does he get that stubborn streak? How
did he learn negativity? When did he start to stand
with his hands on his hips in defiance? My parents
must surely have wondered the same thing when I was
reaching to be my own person.

You didn't wonder, though. You saw my heart and
knew I would reach a time of transformation—when
I gave my life over to You. A change of heart, attitude,
and self still remains for my son. I pray that I may be
able to love him unconditionally as he tries to find
himself and as the day is approaching when he will
give himself over to You.

Storming the Walls

Better a patient man than a warrior,
a man who controls his temper than one who takes
a city.

PROVERBS 16:32

My son wants to be a superhero. He used to wear the capes and tights around the house. Now he just takes on the demeanor of one for special holidays... and when I ask him to clean his room. I know little boys want to be warriors, heroes—they want to storm the walls of the city and claim their victory.

Give my son an opportunity to truly learn the courage and strength that patience requires. Allow him to see boys and men who follow this way of might so that manhood is not viewed as the ultimate power but as the chance to be empowered by Your grace.

Balm for the Spirit

A hot-tempered man stirs up dissension,
but a patient man calms a quarrel.

PROVERBS 15:18

Like a lullaby, Your love comforts a restless spirit. Your hand touches the brow and eases a fever. You replace our impatience with a calmness that remains even when we face difficulties. Lord, You are a balm for the spirit.

I pray my son would come to know Your healing touch personally in his life. I want him to know You so well that his heart would be unable to cause dissension and turmoil. The world is in need of Your power of grace. May my child become a peacemaker all of his days.

A Personal Prayer
for My Son

Choices

Lightbulb

You will pray to him, and he will hear you,
and you will fulfill your vows.
What you decide on will be done,
and light will shine on your ways.

JOB 22:27-28

Before we make choices, before the lightbulb finally goes on above our heads, may we always turn to You in prayer. Facing little and big decisions as a family has helped my son see that we can and should bring all things to You in prayer.

Shed light on the path for my son. When he faces a crossroads, may he see the way of Your will. May he never turn his back on Your way, but always be eager to lift his concerns to Your ears and watch for Your light to lead him.

Did You Hear Me?

Choose life, so that you and your children may live and that you may love the LORD your God, listen to his voice, and hold fast to him.

DEUTERONOMY 30:19-20

I repeat myself to my son over and over. We can be standing next to one another, and if he is focused on something else, anything else, my words slide right over his head. I realize how easily distracted I can be when You are trying to speak words of guidance to me. When I pray for Your will to be done and then turn my attention to whatever glitters and glistens, I am not choosing the life You have for me.

Lord, teach me to listen. Allow me to be an example to my son so that he will always seek Your Word, Your voice, and Your life. May his ears be open to the One who is beside him always.

Our Choices

How much better to get wisdom than gold,
to choose understanding rather than silver!

PROVERBS 16:16

The decisions in my son's life started with simple things like "What do you want to wear today?" and progressed to "Which book do you want to read?" and "Where should we go on vacation?" But I know he will face many choices that are more significant, choices that will require a clear decision and commitment to follow through once the choice is made.

Material pleasures will tempt him along the way. Sometimes they will come in the form of blessings. But other times they will come in the shape of a choice between that which is of the world versus that which is of You and Your plan. May he always seek wisdom and understanding over the riches of the world.

A Personal Prayer for My Son

Humility

After the Fall

When pride comes, then comes disgrace, but with humility comes wisdom.

PROVERBS 11:2

I have tended to the scraped knee of my son after a tumble. I have wiped away tears after a fall. But my heart knows of another injury my child will face—hurt pride. It is the fall that comes into all of our lives at different times. I pray the tumble will not be severe, will not break him, will not destroy his hope.

But whatever does come his way after times of pride, I know You will be there to wipe away his tears and heal him with the gift of humility and the strength of wisdom.

Me First

Do nothing out of selfish ambition or vain conceit,
but in humility consider others better than your-
selves.

PHILIPPIANS 2:3

Oh, how I want my son to have a heart for others.
To truly see the needs and wonders of other individuals. Grant him a heart that expands beyond self and
stretches to include those who can teach him Your
love.

May his worth always be from his identity as Your
child, so that he never has to prove his value in selfish
ways or through blind ambition. Inspire him by leading
him into the presence of those who practice compassion. Teach me to build him up in ways that encourage
humility and righteousness.

Listen to Your Elders

*Young men, in the same way be submissive to those
who are older. All of you, clothe yourselves with
humility toward one another, because, "God opposes
the proud but gives grace to the humble."*

1 PETER 5:5

Everything new and trendy catches the eye of my
son. I worry he will not have respect for the legacy of
the past and the wisdom of his elders. Help me teach
him how to listen to and honor others by the way we
practice these things in our home.

Will he know Your grace is extended to the humble?
Does he see the value in a humble heart and spirit?
May these lessons be learned now as he is growing
so that he will be open to the teachings of those You
place in his path.

A Personal Prayer for My Son

Generosity

A Giving Spirit

*Out of the most severe trial, their overflowing
joy and their extreme poverty welled up in rich
generosity.*

2 CORINTHIANS 8:2

Will my son learn how to find Your joy in difficult circumstances? Will he discover that in times of poverty or sacrifice there is always something he has to offer others through Your grace? Lord, lead my child through circumstances that strengthen his understanding of what it means to be generous and joyful.

Take away those things in our home life that elevate selfishness or wrongful desires. Build up our desire for Your wealth so that we might serve others and realize richness in our poverty. Give my son a heart anchored to You during times of both trial and blessing.

Those Who Follow

Because of the service by which you have proved yourselves, men will praise God for the obedience that accompanies your confession of the gospel of Christ, and for your generosity in sharing with them and with everyone else.

2 CORINTHIANS 9:13

I see signs of leadership in my son. I wonder what You have in store for his career, his path, his passion. May his steps always honor You. I pray his words and deeds would bring You glory so that those who follow him will see Your hand upon his life.

God, express the gospel through my child's life. Remind him he is dependent upon You, the Creator, for all that comes to him—so that when he is generous, he understands he is a steward of Your goodness. Give him the courage to confess his faith so his obedience would lead others to Your feet.

Because He Is Loved

As God's chosen people, holy and dearly loved,
clothe yourselves with compassion, kindness,
humility, gentleness and patience.

COLOSSIANS 3:12

I try to show my son Your love in different ways.
I encourage him and practice forgiveness and faithfulness as best I can. His identity as my son is a blessing
to me—but God, I understand it will be his identity in
You that truly clothes him in goodness. His heart and
spirit will be shaped by Your hand.

Because my son is loved by You, he is able to be
compassionate, kind, gentle, and patient with those he
encounters. And because You love him, I can come to
You today and ask that You would guide him always
in this way of generosity.

A Personal Prayer
for My Son

Life

A Great Love

My son, pay attention to what I say;
listen closely to my words.
Do not let them out of your sight,
keep them within your heart;
for they are life to those who find them
and health to a man's whole body.
Above all else, guard your heart,
for it is the wellspring of life.

PROVERBS 4:20-23

Watch out for false friends. Always stand up for those in need. Be yourself. I pass along wisdom left and right to my son. Sometimes he shrugs it off—other times I know he is listening and filing it away for future use.

But there is a point beyond which my words will exist only as memory or as lessons engraved on my son's heart. My prayer is that I will have raised him to love others and to seek You with all that he has and is. I gave him birth, Lord—but You gave him life. From now on, we are in this great love together.

Other Good
Harvest House Reading

One-Minute Prayers™ for Busy Moms

Whatever the age of your children, you will enjoy this sanctuary of simple prayers and inspirational verses. Amid the scheduled, the unscheduled, and all the other demands of family, a minute with God will free you to find joy in everyday events, see God's reflection in your children, and create a life that feeds your family spiritually.

One-Minute Prayers™

Here's an everyday-life way to bring your needs, concerns, requests, and desires to your Father. Topically arranged prayers and Scripture verses will help you to release worries to Him, define success His way, and praise and thank your Creator in everything.

Battle Plan for Spiritual Warfare
Joe Wasmond and Rich Miller

If you feel spiritually vulnerable in key areas of your life, here's some solid "basic training." In this concise, easy-to-read resource, Joe Wasmond, president of Freedom in Christ Ministries, and Rich Miller use illustrations from Joe's experiences as a pilot in Vietnam to target powerful biblical messages to such topics as...

∞ the role of prayer in providing invisible protection

∞ the armor and abundant supplies God has given us

∞ the need to trust that God is good and wants the best for you

HARVEST HOUSE
PUBLISHERS